Stacey Abrams

Melissa H. Mwai

NATIONAL GEOGRAPHIC

Washington, D.C.

To Lucas, Elise, Nico, and mi familia —M.H.M.

Published by National Geographic Partners, LLC, Washington, DC 20036.

Designed by Gus Tello

Library of Congress Cataloging-in-Publication Data

Names: Mwai, Melissa H., author.
Title: Stacey Abrams / by Melissa H. Mwai.
Description: Washington, D.C. : National Geographic Kids, [2022] | Series: National Geographic readers. Level 2 | Audience: Ages 5-8 | Audience: Grades K-1
Identifiers: LCCN 2021035958 (print) | LCCN 2021035959 (ebook) | ISBN 9781426373268 (trade paperback) | ISBN 9781426373565 (library binding) | ISBN 9781426373480 (ebook other) | ISBN 9781426373497 (ebook)
Subjects: LCSH: Abrams, Stacey--Juvenile literature. | African American women politicians--Georgia--Biography--Juvenile literature. | Politicians--Georgia--Biography--Juvenile literature. | Legislators--Georgia--Biography--Juvenile literature. | Suffrage--United States--History--21st century. | African American legislators--Georgia--Biography--Juvenile literature.
Classification: LCC F291.3.A27 M93 2022 (print) | LCC F291.3.A27 (ebook) | DDC 975.8/044092 [B]--dc23
LC record available at https://lccn.loc .gov/2021035958
LC ebook record available at https://lccn.loc .gov/2021035959

The author and publisher gratefully acknowledge the literacy review of this book by Mariam Jean Dreher, professor emerita of reading education, University of Maryland, College Park, and fact-checking by Michelle Harris.

Photo Credits
AS = Adobe Stock; GI = Getty Images; SS = Shutterstock
Cover, McClatchy-Tribune/Tribune Content Agency LLC/Alamy Stock Photo; header (throughout), spyrakot/AS; vocabulary art (throughout), martialred/AS; 1, Tami Chappell/EPA-EFE/SS; 3, Darryl Brooks/SS; 5, Jessica McGowan/GI; 6, Everett/SS; 7, Steve Schapiro/Corbis via GI; 8 (UP), rodphotography/AS; 8 (LO), Bettmann/GI; 9, Nick Arroyo/Atlanta Journal-Constitution via AP; 10 (LE), John Bazemore/AP/SS; 10 (RT), AlenKadr/AS; 11 (UP RT), NAACP via GI; 11 (LO LE), Pool via AP; 12, Nick Arroyo/Atlanta Journal-Constitution via AP; 13, Liderina/SS; 14, Jessica McGowan/GI; 14-15, andreykr/AS; 16, David Goldman/AP/SS; 17, AP Photo/John Amis; 18, Melina Mara/The Washington Post via GI; 19, Alyssa Pointer/ Atlanta Journal-Constitution via AP; 20, Bob Andres/Atlanta Journal-Constitution via AP; 21 (LE), ZUMA Press, Inc./Alamy Live News; 21 (RT), C.B. Schmelter/Chattanooga Times Free Press via AP; 22 (UP LE), Bastiaan Slabbers/NurPhoto via GI; 22 (UP RT), Sadayuki Mikami/AP/SS; 22 (LO), Copyright C-SPAN; 23 (UP LE), Jaroslav Kruševskij/AS; 23 (UP RT), Copyright 2021 NBAE-Photo by Adam Hagy/NBAE via GI; 23 (LO), Elijah Nouvelage for The Washington Post via GI; 24-25, C.B. Schmelter/Chattanooga Times Free Press via AP; 25, Bill Oxford/GI; 26-29 (timeline), santima.studio/AS; 27, Melina Mara/ The Washington Post via GI; 28, Melina Mara/ The Washington Post via GI; 29 (both), Elijah Nouvelage/GI; 30 (LE), John Bazemore/AP/SS; 30 (RT), Bettmann/GI; 31 (UP LE), Jessica McGowan/GI; 31 (UP RT), Tatiana/AS; 31 (LO), Dustin Chambers/GI; 32 (UP LE), Jessica McGowan/GI; 32 (UP RT), John Spink/Atlanta Journal-Constitution via AP; 32 (CTR LE), andreykr/AS; 32 (CTR RT), Tami Chappell/EPA-EFE/SS; 32 (LO LE), John Bazemore/AP/SS; 32 (LO RT), Yale University Art Gallery

Printed in the United States of America
21/WOR/1

Contents

Meet Stacey Abrams

It was 2018 in Georgia, U.S.A., and people were angry. Problems had made it hard to vote. Some people could not vote on election (ee-LEK-shun) day. But every voice matters in an election.

So Stacey Abrams took action. She used her words to help make sure people could vote. Her stories sparked change.

Words to KNOW

ELECTION: Voting to choose government leaders

4

Abrams marching with voters during the 2018 election

In Her Own WORDS

"Everything I do is bounded by this commitment my parents instilled in me. I can't just see a problem, I've got the job to fix it."

Unfair Treatment

Less than 10 years before Abrams was born, people in some states had to take tests or pay money to vote. That stopped many people, especially Black people, from voting. People protested. Many were hurt, arrested, or killed.

Protesters in 1965 outside the White House in Washington, D.C.

Protesters march to Selma, Alabama, U.S.A., in 1985 to support voting rights.

The protests worked. In 1965, a new law said that tests or money could no longer be used to stop people from voting. But some people still treated Black people unfairly.

Atlanta, Georgia

When Abrams was 16, her family moved from Mississippi to Atlanta, Georgia.

At Abrams's new school, the students with the best grades were invited to the governor's house. Abrams was invited! At first, she was stopped by a guard. She thought it was because of the color of her skin.

The Georgia governor's house in Atlanta

Abrams did go in, but she was upset that she was treated differently from the other students. That fall, Abrams started college. She decided to use her studies to fight for fair treatment.

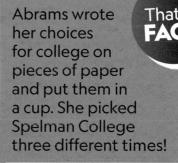

Abrams wrote her choices for college on pieces of paper and put them in a cup. She picked Spelman College three different times!

That's a
FACT!

Abrams as a student at Spelman College in Atlanta

Abrams's Cool Firsts

Stacey Abrams was the first to do a lot of things. Did you know these firsts?

1 **Stacey Abrams** was the **first Black woman** to be **nominated** for governor by a major political party, Democrats or Republicans. The governor is the **highest leader in the state.**

2 Abrams was the **first lawyer** in her family.

3

In 2021, the NAACP gave its **first** ever **Social Justice Impact Award** to Abrams. **The NAACP is a group that fights for equal rights.**

4

Abrams was the **first Black woman** to give the State of the Union response.

Words to **KNOW**

VOTE

NOMINATE: To recommend for a job or award

STATE OF THE UNION: A speech given each year by the president of the United States about things the president thinks are important

Finding Her Voice

Abrams giving a speech as student vice president at Spelman College

Abrams believed the best way to fight for change was to become a school leader. So Abrams ran for student vice president at Spelman College.

Abrams was shy. But she practiced her speeches. That helped her feel less shy. Before she could give them, though, other students stole them all. What could she do now? Abrams wrote new speeches—and won!

Words to KNOW

VOTE

RUN: To campaign, or try to be elected

13

Speaking for Atlanta

Abrams attended more schools to learn to be a better leader. Finally, she became a lawyer for the city of Atlanta. Part of her job was to help write a plan to set up voting places.

People signing in to vote

Abrams wanted to do even more. In 2006, she ran for Georgia's House of Representatives. Abrams met with her neighbors. She told them her plans to make Georgia a fairer place to live. She won the election.

The Georgia capitol building in Atlanta

Words to KNOW

HOUSE OF REPRESENTATIVES: A group of state leaders, called representatives, who work with state senators to write laws

15

As a representative, Abrams spoke for the people in her district. The people wanted more money for preschools. So Abrams talked with other leaders. She asked them to help. They agreed and passed a new law.

Soon after, Abrams wanted to run for governor. By being in charge, she could help the whole state—not just the families in her district.

Words to KNOW

DISTRICT: An area of a state that elects a leader to represent it

That's a **FACT!**

Abrams wrote so many laws that other representatives asked her for help writing their laws, too!

Georgia governor Nathan Deal signing Abrams's law to support preschools

The Race for Governor

To help people vote during the election, Abrams set up a phone number. Anyone could call to share their problems voting. More than 50,000 people called.

Difficulty Voting?

Talk to Me

or call

If you think you're registered and been denied a vote, you can cast a provisional ballot.

Some people said they could not vote because their voting place had run out of paper.

Others were turned away because they had the wrong ID cards. And some people had been removed from the voting lists.

Waiting in long lines during Georgia's 2018 election

On November 6, 2018, the people of Georgia voted for their new governor. Abrams lost. Losing the governor's race upset Abrams.

But hearing stories about unfair voting problems upset her even more. That same day, Abrams started a group called Fair Fight. Her new group would share people's stories about voting problems. She hoped their stories would help to change laws.

6 COOL Facts About Abrams

1

Abrams writes books, too! Her first novel was **published** in 2001.

Minority Leader
HOW TO LEAD FROM THE OUTSIDE AND MAKE REAL CHANGE

STACEY ABRAMS

2

In college, Abrams was the **only student** to **work** with Atlanta's **mayor.**

3

On August 28, 1993, Abrams gave her **first big speech.** It was **given** on the same day as **Martin Luther King, Jr.'s famous speech** in Washington, D.C., 30 years earlier.

STACY ABRAMS
YOUTH SPEAKER

CH 71   08-28-93   14

4

Abrams has **started many businesses.** One made ready-to-serve **baby bottles.**

5

Abrams **helped start** the Women's National Basketball Association (WNBA) **team** called the **Atlanta Dream.**

6

As a teen, Abrams started **a list of goals** that she still uses today. **One goal** was to be **a millionaire!**

Helping Voices Count

In 2019, Abrams started Fair Count. This group helped people fill out the 2020 census (SEN-sis). The census tells the government facts about who lives in each state.

Those facts help
the government
know how many
districts each
state should have
and how many leaders
should represent each state.

The 2020 census form

Abrams asks a crowd to join in her fight for fair voting.

Fair Fight helped more people know how and where to vote. Usually, most people vote in person. But during the 2020 election, many people were scared about a sickness called COVID-19. They avoided crowds.

Abrams gave speeches. She told people to vote by mail or vote early. She wanted everyone to know about the different ways they could vote and stay safe from the sickness.

1973
Born in Madison, Wisconsin, U.S.A., on December 9

1991
Attends Spelman College in Atlanta

1993
Delivers speech at the anniversary of Dr. King's March on Washington

That's a FACT! More Americans voted in the 2020 election than in any other in U.S. history.

1999
Graduates from Yale Law School

2001
Publishes first book

2003
Works as deputy city attorney in Atlanta

Lift Every Voice

Abrams may have lost the governor's race, but her words had helped others. This shy girl became a leader who helped millions of people's votes and voices be heard.

2007
Sworn in as Georgia state representative on January 8

2010
Becomes the first Black female minority leader in Georgia's House of Representatives

2018
Becomes the first Black woman nominated for governor on May 22

In Her Own WORDS

"My goal is to not only have the ability to lift up the families in my state, but to redefine our beliefs in who can lead."

Abrams's story inspires us to speak up when we want things to change. She is still fighting for fairness, because every voice counts.

2018
Ends governor's race and starts Fair Fight on November 16

2019
Starts Fair Count

2021
Wins the NAACP Social Justice Impact Award for voting rights

QUIZ WHIZ

How much do you know about Stacey Abrams? After reading this book, probably a lot! Take this quiz and find out.

Answers are at the bottom of p. 31.

1 Stacey Abrams was the _____ Black woman in U.S. history nominated for governor by a major political party.

A. last
B. first
C. third

2 In which state did Abrams visit the governor's house in high school?

A. Wisconsin
B. Mississippi
C. Georgia
D. Texas

3 While a student at Spelman College, Abrams worked with the mayor of Atlanta.

A. true
B. false

4 After Abrams was done with school, she became _____ .

A. mayor of Atlanta
B. a lawyer for Atlanta
C. state representative in New York
D. all of the above

5 During the 2018 election, Abrams set up a phone line so people could share stories about voting problems.

A. true
B. false

6 Which voting problems did Abrams think were unfair?

A. having the wrong ID card
B. being taken off voting lists
C. voting by mail
D. both A and B

7 What are the names of the two organizations that Abrams started to help voters?

A. Atlanta and Dream
B. Fair Fight and Fair Count
C. Democrat and Republican
D. District and Census

Answers: 1. B, 2. C, 3. A, 4. B, 5. A, 6. D, 7. B

31

GLOSSARY

DISTRICT: An area of a state that elects a leader to represent it

ELECTION: Voting to choose government leaders

HOUSE OF REPRESENTATIVES: A group of state leaders, called representatives, who work with state senators to write laws

NOMINATE: To recommend for a job or award

RUN: To campaign, or try to be elected

STATE OF THE UNION: A speech given each year by the president of the United States about things the president thinks are important

32